W9-BUY-393

Can You Find These Rocks?

Carmen Bredeson and Lindsey Cousins

Enslow Elementary
an imprint of
Enslow Publishers, Inc.

40 Industrial Road
Box 398
Berkeley Heights, NJ 07922
USA

http://www.enslow.com

Enslow Elementary, an imprint of Enslow Publishers, Inc.
Enslow Elementary® is a registered trademark of Enslow Publishers, Inc.

Library of Congress Cataloging-in-Publication Data
Bredeson, Carmen.
  Can you find these rocks? / Carmen Bredeson and Lindsey Cousins.
    p. cm. — (All about nature)
  Includes index.
  Summary: "Introduces pre-readers to simple concepts about rocks using short sentences and repetition of words"—Provided by publisher.
  ISBN 978-0-7660-3979-7
  1. Rocks—Juvenile literature. 2. Rocks—Identification—Juvenile literature. I. Cousins, Lindsey. II. Title.
  QE432.2.B738 2012
  552—dc23
                              2011028394

Future editions:
Paperback ISBN 978-1-4644-0066-7
ePUB ISBN 978-1-4645-0973-5
PDF ISBN 978-1-4646-0973-2

Printed in China
012012 Leo Paper Group, Heshan City, Guangdong, China
10 9 8 7 6 5 4 3 2 1

To Our Readers: We have done our best to make sure all Internet Addresses in this book were active and appropriate when we went to press. However, the author and the publisher have no control over and assume no liability for the material available on those Internet sites or on other Web sites they may link to. Any comments or suggestions can be sent by e-mail to comments@enslow.com or to the address on the back cover.

Photo Credits: Shutterstock.com
Cover Photo: © 2011 Photos.com, a division of Getty Images. All rights reserved.

Note to Parents and Teachers
Help pre-readers get a jump start on reading. These lively stories introduce simple concepts with repetition of words and short simple sentences. Photos and illustrations fill the pages with color and effectively enhance the text. Free Educator Guides are available for this series at www.enslow.com. Search for the *All About Nature* series name.

Contents

Words to Know

arrowhead
(AR oh hed)

vinegar
(VIH nih gur)

volcano
(vahl KAY noh)

3

Rocks

It is easy to find rocks.

You can find rocks in your yard.

You can find rocks in the park.

Rocks are all around us.

Some rocks are little.

Some rocks are big.

Rocks are many colors.

Can you find some of the rocks in

this book?

Pumice

Pumice (PUH miss) has a

lot of little holes.

It is not very heavy.

Throw a piece of pumice

in the water.

Watch it float! It does not sink.

Sandstone

Sandstone is made
from a lot of sand.
The sand piles up.
The sand on the top
presses down hard.
The sand on the bottom
turns to rock.
It takes a long time for sand
to turn to sandstone.

Slate

Slate is flat and shiny.

It is made of many thin layers.

Slate is good for making floors.

Many people make walking

paths with slate.

Look where you walk.

It may be a slate floor or path.

Basalt

Basalt is cool lava.

Lava comes out of *volcanoes*.

The lava starts out very hot.

When it cools off it

becomes basalt.

Basalt can be

black or grey.

It can be found

all over the world.

Marble

Marble can be found in many places.

A lot of statues are made out of marble.

Some people even live in marble houses.

Marble can do something cool.

Dip a piece of marble in some *vinegar*.

The rock will bubble a little.

Granite

Granite is a
very hard rock.
It is used to make
a lot of things.
Many buildings are
made out of granite.
Some mountains are granite.
Granite has many spots of color.
The spots will help you find it.

Limestone

Limestone is made

in the ocean.

Old shells fall to

the bottom of the ocean.

Some little sea animals fall there too.

They are all mashed together.

After a long time they turn

into limestone.

Look for pieces of shells in rock.

It may be limestone.

Flint

Flint is not
very strong.
Hit a piece of

flint with another rock. It chips.

You can chip flint into many shapes.

People used to make

tools out of flint.

A long time ago they

made *arrowheads*.

What would you make out of flint?

Chalk

Chalk is a

very soft rock.

It is easy to break.

You can write with it too.

Find a piece of chalk rock.

Rub it on a sidewalk.

It will leave markings behind.

Draw pictures of some rocks on

the sidewalk.

Read More

Kompelien, Tracy. *Cool Rocks*. Edina, Minn.: ABDO Publishing Co., 2007.

Rosinsky, Natalie M. *Rocks: Hard, Soft, Smooth, and Rough*. Mankato, Minn.: Picture Window Books, 2006.

Wallace, Nancy Elizabeth. *Rocks! Rocks! Rocks!* Tarrytown, N.Y.: Marshall Cavendish, 2009.

Web Sites

Children's Museum of Indianapolis. <www.childrensmuseum.org/geomysteries/faqs.html>

National Geographic Kids. <http://kids.nationalgeographic.com/kids/activities/funscience/rock-on>

Index

Guided Reading Level: E
Guided Reading Leveling System is based on the guidelines recommended by Fountas and Pinnell.

Word Count: 398